THE SACRED JOURNEY

SELF-CARE STRATEGIES FOR WOMEN OVER 50

JOLISA WEBB DUDLEY

THE SACRED JOURNEY:
SELF-CARE STRATEGIES FOR WOMEN OVER 50

BY JOLISA WEBB DUDLEY

© 2025 Jolisa Webb Dudley

Beauty in the Midst Publishing

ISBN: 979-8-9992194-0-4

All rights reserved. No part of this book may be reproduced, stored in a retrieval system, or transmitted in any form or by any means—electronic, mechanical, photocopying, recording, or otherwise—without the prior written permission of the publisher.

This book is for informational and inspirational purposes only. It is not intended to replace professional medical, psychological, legal, or financial advice. Always seek the advice of a qualified professional regarding your personal situation.

Publishing consulting services provided by Dr. Matt Deaton of Notaed Press.

Back cover photo by Roy Cox of Roy Cox Photography. Photoshoot support provided by Tia Richardson of Lavish Beauty Suites and Keaira Bright of Keaira Makeup Artistry.

Scripture quotations are from the Holy Bible, New International Version® (NIV®), unless otherwise noted.

Dedication

For every woman who has ever felt invisible in her own story—this is your invitation to come home to yourself.

For the ones who gave so much, they forgot they were allowed to receive.
For the ones who kept showing up with grace, even when no one clapped.
For the soft-hearted warriors, the silent prayers, the quiet comebacks.
For the women navigating change with trembling hands and unshakeable faith—I see you. I honor you. This book was written with you in mind.

May these pages remind you that you are not behind.
You are not broken.
You are the answered prayer, becoming the next chapter of someone's healing—and your own.

Hey, Beautiful… I see you, because I am you.

Acknowledgments

Thank you, Dr. Matt Deaton, Notaed Press, for being more than an editor—for being a trusted thought partner in this sacred undertaking. Your care, your presence, and your belief in the vision behind this book helped me feel seen, supported, and strengthened every step of the way

Special thanks to Roy Cox, Roy Cox Photography for the stunning photography that captured the spirit of this season so beautifully. Deeply grateful also for my amazing glam team Tia Richardson, Lavish Beauty Suites and Keaira Bright, Keaira Makeup Artistry for your artistry, care, and presence behind the scenes—you helped me feel radiant, grounded, and powerful in front of the lens.

Last, thank you to my generous and kind beta readers, Audra Griner, KC McClain, and Stephanie Sutton-Johnson. Your thoughtful feedback made this book so much better. I'm forever indebted.

Note from the Author

Self-care isn't selfish, it's sacred.™

This book was born from that truth.

We've been taught to see self-care as indulgence—or worse, as something optional. But what if it's actually a divine responsibility? What if caring for your whole self—body, mind, spirit, emotions, purpose, and rest—is one of the most sacred things you'll ever do?

To be sacred is to be set apart, protected, cherished, and holy. It's a word that has been whispered in scripture, carried through generations, and often misunderstood. In the context of this book, sacred means honoring the divine within you. It means creating space for restoration, alignment, and reverence—not just in grand gestures, but in the quiet, everyday choices that bring you home to yourself.

"He restores my soul." — Psalm 23:3

This verse from Psalm 23 has held me through many seasons. It reminds me that the act of restoring the soul is God's idea. Sacred self-care is not a trend or a luxury—it is a spiritual practice. It is how we partner with God to become whole again.

In a world that glorifies hustle, numbs grief, and overlooks women in transition, choosing to care for your soul is a radical, holy act.

The Sacred Journey invites you to explore self-care not as a task to complete, but as a way of being. You'll walk through real-life milestones—marriage, widowhood, divorce, caregiving, menopause, aging, and rediscovery—with compassion and clarity. Each chapter offers heartfelt reflections, soul-centered practices, and space for legacy thinking, because your story matters. Your healing matters. Your wholeness matters.

You'll also find a Sacred Self-Care Toolkit at the end of the book. This includes a deeper exploration of the six core types of self-care to help guide you along the way. You don't need to memorize them—you'll feel them. As you read, your spirit will recognize what needs tending.

Above all, let this be a gentle guide, not a rigid plan. This is your sacred journey. And it begins with a single breath.

This book was written with deep reflection, lived experience, and love. While I used trusted tools and support along the way—including thoughtful editorial collaboration and creative assistance—every word has been guided by my heart, my faith, and my own sacred journey. I pray it reaches you with the same intention in which it was written.

Table of Contents

Dedication i
Note from the Author iii
Preface: Honoring Life's Milestones Through Sacred Self-Care 1
Introduction: Embracing the Sacredness of Self-Care 3
This Book Will Wait for You 5

Part I
Sacred Transitions:
Honoring Life's Defining Shifts

Chapter 1 Marriage, Love, and Sacred Boundaries 9

Chapter 2 Life After Loss: Widowhood, Grief, and Grace 15

Chapter 3 Empty Nest, Full Heart 21

Chapter 4 Divorce, Grief, and New Beginnings 27

Chapter 5 The Sacred Shift: Menopause with Grace 33

Chapter 6 Redefining Success: Retirement and Career Transitions 39

Chapter 7 The Evolving Circle: When Friendships Fade 45

Chapter 8 Caregiving as a Sacred Calling ..53

Part II
Sacred Wholeness:
Returning to Yourself

Chapter 9 Vitality Reimagined 63

Chapter 10 Emotional Resilience 69

Chapter 11 Sacred Alignment 75

Chapter 12 Rediscovering You 81

Chapter 13 Love at Every Stage 89

Part III
Sacred Legacy:
Living and Leaving a Life That Teaches

Chapter 14 Life in Harmony 97

Chapter 15 Living Sacredly Through Life's Seasons 103

Closing Reflections: You Are the Sacred Journey 109

Book Club Questions 113

Sacred Self-Care Toolkit 115

About the Author 121

Preface
Honoring Life's Milestones Through Sacred Self-Care

There are moments in life that change us forever.

Some arrive softly—like a new love, a second chance, or a quiet breakthrough. Others crash in like waves—divorce, death, betrayal, menopause, or an unexpected transition that cracks us wide open.

What I've learned is this: Every milestone, even the painful ones, offers an invitation. To reset. To reclaim. To remember that your needs are not a burden—they are a birthright.

As women, we often carry the emotional and spiritual weight of those around us. We mother, partner, lead, protect, serve, and sacrifice. But we are not only here to pour—we are also here to be filled. Sacred self-care is how we begin again, no matter what season we're in.

This book is a companion for those in the thick of transition—whether you're navigating the silence of widowhood, the overwhelm of caregiving, or the soft power of rediscovering yourself after 50. It's also for those who simply want to live more intentionally, with wisdom and grace.

As you walk through each chapter, know this: You are not alone. You are seen, held, and divinely supported.

Let this be a sacred unfolding.

Introduction
Embracing the Sacredness of Self-Care

This book is not a how-to—it's a heart-to.
It doesn't follow rigid rules or conventional formatting. Instead, it offers room to breathe. To reflect. To return to yourself.

The writing flows like a sacred conversation between sisters. You may find short paragraphs, poetic pauses, and unexpected whitespace. That's not a glitch—it's an invitation.

Self-care isn't selfish, it's sacred. ™

That's more than a catchphrase—it's a quiet revolution.

For too long, women have been praised for how much we carry, how well we perform, and how often we pour. But sacred self-care calls us back to ourselves. It invites us to rest, to remember, and to reclaim the parts of us that got lost in the noise of survival.

This book isn't about bubble baths or trendy checklists. It's about truth. It's about how we care for our spirits, our bodies, and our hearts in seasons of transition, uncertainty, and rebirth.

Whether you're navigating a new chapter or healing from an old one, let this be a reminder that your well-being is not optional—it's foundational.

Throughout this journey, we'll explore sacred self-care through three main sections: Transitions, Wholeness, and Legacy. Each chapter holds space for real life, real emotions, and real healing.

Sacred self-care is not a one-time fix—it's a lifelong relationship with yourself. And you, beloved, are worthy of that care.

Let's begin.

This Book Will Wait for You

A note for your spirit.

We first whispered this in the introduction, but it bears repeating—slowly, sacredly, and on its own page:

This book will wait for you.

It will wait while you pause to catch your breath.
It will wait while you cry, or pray, or take a nap.
It will wait while you live—while you care for others, or stare at the ceiling, or walk outside to feel the sun on your face.

It was written with your humanity in mind.

You are not behind. You are not broken. You are not failing if you need to read this one paragraph at a time or put it down and come back months later. That's not avoidance—it's wisdom.

Healing doesn't happen on a schedule.
Neither does clarity.
And neither does God.

There will be chapters that meet you in your now.
Others will speak to your next.
And some may simply be seeds that bloom when the season is right.

We included this note because it matters that much.
Your rest matters that much.
Your presence, not your pace, is what carries you forward.

So breathe. Pause. Re-read. Or wait.
This book will be right here when you're ready—no guilt, no rush, no rules.

Because healing is sacred. And so are you.

Love and Light,
Jolisa

PART I

SACRED TRANSITIONS: HONORING LIFE'S DEFINING Shifts

Chapter 1
Marriage, Love, and Sacred Boundaries

"I didn't fall in love; I rose in it." — Toni Morrison

Marriage in midlife is not the same as it was in our 20s or 30s. It comes with new rhythms, deeper truths, and often unspoken griefs. The children are grown. The noise quiets. And suddenly, we're left facing the person we married—or who's no longer there—with fresh eyes and unfamiliar silence.

For many women over 50, marriage becomes a mirror. Not just a reflection of love or companionship, but a reflection of who we've become, what we've endured, and how we've changed.

Some marriages deepen. Others dissolve. And still others quietly coast, leaving both partners wondering if this is all there is.

But here's the sacred truth: Marriage at this stage is an invitation—not a destination.

It's an invitation to:
- Relearn each other
- Reclaim your individuality

- Redefine what connection and intimacy look like now
- Honor the sacred boundaries needed to love fully without losing yourself

Self-Care Within Marriage

Whether you've been married for 5 years or 45, self-care must be part of the union. Without it, resentment builds, communication erodes, and softness becomes exhaustion.

Sacred self-care in marriage means:

- Speaking your needs without apology
- Reclaiming joy for yourself, not waiting for permission
- Creating space for companionship and solitude
- Setting boundaries that protect your peace, not punish your partner
- Praying together, but also praying for yourself

When the Marriage Shifts

Some women reading this are still married. Others are separated. Others are grieving a love that ended, emotionally or legally. Some are remarried—or preparing to love again.

Wherever you fall, know this:

You are not defined by your relationship status. You are defined by how you love, how you live, and how you care for the woman within.

Let this chapter be a sacred pause—a space to reflect, not judge. Whether your marriage is thriving, treading water, or long behind you, you are still sacred. And the care you offer yourself now will shape how you love and connect in every relationship moving forward.

Scripture

> *"Above all, love each other deeply, because love covers over a multitude of sins."* — 1 Peter 4:8

This scripture reminds us that love, in all its forms—romantic, self-directed, divine—requires depth, intention, and grace. It calls us to lead with compassion, even when navigating hard truths or setting sacred boundaries.

Thinking About Legacy

If your daughter, son, or grandchildren watched how you love and set boundaries today, what would they learn? Would they see love rooted in truth and tenderness? Would they understand that self-respect is a sacred act? How can your current relationship choices model a new way of loving—with faith, honesty, and self-awareness?

Reflection Prompts

1. What boundaries in my relationships honor both love and my well-being?
2. How have I grown in how I express or receive love over the years?
3. What does "sacred connection" look like to me now?
4. Am I tending to my relationship with myself as tenderly as I tend to others?

Sacred Reflections: Your Notes

The Sacred Journey

Marriage, Love, and Sacred Boundaries

Chapter 2
Life After Loss: Widowhood, Grief, and Grace

"Grief, I've learned, is really just love. It's all the love you want to give but cannot. All of that unspent love gathers in the corners of your eyes, the lump in your throat, and in that hollow part of your chest." — Jamie Anderson

There is a silence that follows death—a silence unlike any other. It isn't just the absence of a voice or the stillness of an empty chair. It's the absence of rhythm. Of shared routines. Of a hand that once reached for yours in the middle of the night.

Widowhood is a word no one prepares for. Even when it comes after illness. Even when you knew the moment was near. It still arrives like a thief, stealing not only your partner but the version of yourself that existed in the context of that love.

For many women, grief is not linear. It comes in waves. One moment you're remembering a shared joke, the next you're frozen in the grocery store because you passed their favorite snack. Sometimes, the loss hits loud and hard.

Other times, it lingers quietly, a gentle ache that never fully leaves.

But here is the sacred truth:
Widowhood is not the end of your story. It is the beginning of a new chapter—one you didn't ask for, but one that still holds grace.

You are not betraying their memory by living again. You honor it with every breath you choose to take fully. Every laugh. Every new experience. Every act of courage.

As one of my coaching clients shared, "I didn't just lose my husband. I lost the version of myself I was with him. And slowly, with God's help, I've had to meet myself all over again."

This chapter is a quiet honoring of that process. Of the healing. Of the mess. Of the joy that eventually peeks through the cracks of sorrow.

Self-Care Through Grief

Self-care after loss looks different. It is not bubble baths and spa days. It is breathwork and bravery. It is spiritual tenderness and fierce grace.

Sacred self-care might include:
- Saying their name out loud—even when others avoid it
- Letting yourself grieve without apology
- Refusing to rush your healing for anyone's comfort

- Seeking support from grief counselors, spiritual guides, or trusted friends
- Creating rituals to honor their memory and your ongoing life
- Laughing when the moment comes—and not feeling guilty when it does

Grief may never leave, but neither does love. You carry both now—hand in hand, heart in heart.

Scripture

"The Lord is close to the brokenhearted and saves those who are crushed in spirit." — Psalm 34:18

This verse is a balm for the grieving soul. It reminds us that God is not distant from our sorrow. He draws near in the quiet, in the tears, and in the sacred rebuilding of life after loss.

Thinking About Legacy

If your children or loved ones watched how you walk through this grief, what would they learn?
Would they see that love doesn't die—it transforms?
Would they witness that tears are holy and joy is still allowed?
Would they learn that grace is not the absence of pain, but the courage to live with it?

Reflection Prompts

1. What have I learned about myself through this season of loss?
2. How can I honor their memory while also honoring my life?
3. What grief have I hidden—and what do I need to let myself feel?
4. Where have I seen God in the midst of my sorrow?

Sacred Reflections: Your Notes

_____

_____

_____

_____

_____

_____

_____

_____

_____

_____

_____

_____

The Sacred Journey

Life After Loss: Widowhood, Grief, and Grace

Chapter 3
Empty Nest, Full Heart

"There are two lasting bequests we can give our children. One is roots. The other is wings."
— Hodding Carter

There comes a moment, often quietly and without warning, when you realize the house has changed. Not just in sound—but in spirit. The lunchboxes are gone. The carpool chaos is over. And the whirlwind of teenage years has faded into phone calls, visits, and memories.

This is the empty nest.

But if we're being honest, it's not always empty. The pantry may be stocked, the schedule wide open—but the heart? The heart is full. Full of pride. Full of questions. Full of unspoken grief for the chapter that just closed.

For many women over 50, this transition is layered. Parenting was the heartbeat of their days. Now, in its absence, some feel relief. Others feel lost. Most feel a blend of both.

When my daughter Rachel left for Howard, I was excited—so proud of her and so ready to cheer her on. But once the adrenaline faded, reality crept in. I looked around my four-bedroom home and realized it was just me and Mimi, our little Yorkie. The silence wasn't peaceful—it echoed. And in that echo was a question I hadn't asked in years: Now what?

But here's the sacred invitation:
This season isn't about loss. It's about rediscovery.

It's about:

- Reconnecting with the woman you were before motherhood became your identity
- Reclaiming your time, voice, and dreams without guilt
- Allowing your relationship with your child to evolve with grace
- Honoring that love still lives here—it just looks different now

Self-Care in the Empty Nest

Self-care in this season asks different questions. Not "What do they need from me?" but "What do I need from myself?"

Sacred self-care might include:

- Redecorating a room not for practicality, but for pleasure
- Traveling alone—or with friends who bring you joy
- Sitting in stillness without rushing to fill the space
- Creating new rituals that center you, not them

- Exploring passions that were paused while raising others

And sometimes, it's letting yourself cry. Not because something is wrong—but because something sacred ended. And your tears are just love leaving the body in a different form.

Scripture

> *"To everything there is a season, and a time to every purpose under the heaven."* — Ecclesiastes 3:1

This verse reminds us that transitions are not mistakes—they are rhythms. The season of active mothering may shift, but your purpose, your love, and your presence still matter deeply. They just take new shape.

Thinking About Legacy

If your child watched how you navigated this new chapter, what would they learn?
Would they learn that letting go can be an act of love?
Would they see that mothers are women, too—with dreams, needs, and sacred paths?
Would they feel permission to grow—and keep coming home in their own way?

Reflection Prompts

1. Who am I now that my role as a hands-on parent has shifted?
2. What brings me joy that has nothing to do with caregiving or being needed?
3. Where am I resisting this transition—and what might happen if I surrendered?
4. What sacred rituals can I create to honor both my child's growth and my own?

Sacred Reflections: Your Notes

_____
_____
_____
_____
_____
_____
_____
_____
_____
_____
_____

The Sacred Journey

Empty Nest, Full Heart

Chapter 4
Divorce, Grief, and New Beginnings

"When two people decide to get a divorce, it isn't a sign that they 'don't understand' one another, but a sign that they have, at least, begun to." — Helen Rowland

Divorce after 50 carries a weight that's different. It's not just about the loss of a relationship—it's the grief of losing shared dreams, the home you built, the years you gave, and sometimes even the identity you held within it.

There is no easy way to untangle a life that's been woven together with someone else's. Even when the decision brings peace, the process brings pain. Divorce in midlife is rarely impulsive. It's often the result of years spent trying, praying, sacrificing—and finally, surrendering.

We saw this play out publicly when Al and Tipper Gore divorced after 40 years of marriage. There was no scandal, no betrayal—just two people who had grown in different directions. It stunned many, but it also held up a mirror: sometimes, love evolves. And sometimes, endings come not because something went wrong—but because something sacred shifted.

But here's the sacred reframe:
Divorce is not just an ending. It is also an awakening.

It is the holy ground where grief and grace meet. Where silence turns into clarity. Where the pieces you once gave away slowly return to you, one sacred breath at a time.

This chapter is not about blame. It's about becoming.

It's about:

- Honoring the grief without letting it define you
- Holding space for the anger, without letting it consume you
- Letting go, without hardening your heart
- Making peace with what was, and permission for what could still be

Self-Care After Divorce

Sacred self-care after divorce includes:

- Giving yourself permission to rest and not rush
- Letting others support you without shame
- Rediscovering joy in solitude and spaciousness
- Rebuilding your rituals—daily, spiritual, and practical
- Speaking kindly to yourself, especially on the hard days

You don't need to "bounce back." You're not a rubber band. You are a woman becoming whole in real time. And your softness is not weakness—its wisdom wrapped in tenderness.

Scripture

"Behold, I am doing a new thing; now it springs forth, do you not perceive it?" — Isaiah 43:19

This scripture reminds us that even in endings, God is working. A new season is always in bloom—often quietly, often painfully—but always with purpose. Your story is not over. It's being rewritten with grace.

Thinking About Legacy

If your daughter, son, niece/nephew, or grandchildren saw how you handled heartbreak, what would they learn?
Would they learn that healing is holy?
Would they see that endings can be sacred, too?
Would they witness the quiet courage it takes to begin again?

Reflection Prompts
1. What parts of myself did I lose—or forget—in that relationship?
2. What does healing look like for me now?
3. Where am I still grieving, and where am I ready to grow?
4. What would it mean to give myself permission to begin again?

Sacred Reflections: Your Notes

_____
_____
_____
_____
_____
_____
_____
_____
_____
_____
_____

The Sacred Journey

Divorce, Grief, and New Beginnings

Chapter 5
The Sacred Shift: Menopause with Grace

"I'm not going to be who I was, and I'm not yet who I will be. But I am still becoming—and that is sacred."
— Anonymous

There is a moment in every woman's life when her body stops whispering and starts declaring. Cycles change. Emotions swell. Sleep shifts. And suddenly, we find ourselves standing in a space no one fully prepared us for.

This is menopause. And it is not a curse.

It is a sacred shift—a recalibration of the body, mind, and spirit.

But too often, society treats it like a vanishing. As if women in their 50s are supposed to disappear—fade quietly while their bodies sweat, ache, and rage in silence.

No more. This chapter of your life is not a crisis. It is a calling. An invitation to honor:

- Your body's wisdom
- Your voice's power

- Your spirit's timing
- Your right to rest, rage, rejoice—and rise
- You are not breaking down. You are breaking open.

Self-Care in the Sacred Shift

Menopause is not just physical. It's spiritual, emotional, relational. And because of that, your self-care must become more intentional, more attuned, more holy.

For me, it crept in like fog—so slowly I didn't even recognize it at first. I wasn't sure if I was just tired… or stressed… or maybe both. But once I named it—menopause—oh, she made herself right at home. The symptoms came on like a full-blown house party: hot flashes, night sweats, itchy skin, mood swings, and weight that seemed to appear overnight.

It felt like all the "Seven Dwarfs of Menopause" came marching through—Sweaty, Sleepy, Bloated, Moody, Itchy, Forgetful, and All-Dried-Up. And let me tell you, they did not knock first.

But here's the sacred reframe: I wasn't falling apart—I was being remade. My body wasn't betraying me. It was initiating me. Calling me deeper into wisdom, softness, and surrender.

Sacred self-care in this season might include:

- Saying "no" faster—and without guilt
- Honoring fatigue as a message, not a flaw
- Dressing in what feels good, not what fits the mold

- Nourishing your body with foods and rhythms that support hormonal change
- Using cooling cloths, personal fans, prayer, music, and movement as daily medicine
- Refusing to let this season be defined by shame or invisibility

And when the night sweats come or the tears surprise you, let grace meet you there. You are not less of a woman. You are becoming more of who you were always meant to be.

Scripture

"She is clothed with strength and dignity; she can laugh at the days to come." — Proverbs 31:25

This verse reminds us that strength and dignity don't come from how young we look or how much we endure in silence. They come from how we embrace change with reverence, humor, and holy boldness. Laughter is sacred, even in the midst of hot flashes.

Thinking About Legacy

If your daughter or granddaughter watched how you navigated menopause, what would they learn?
Would they see that aging is not shameful—but sacred?
Would they learn that their bodies are wise, not broken?
Would they see that wholeness comes from self-trust, not youth?

Reflection Prompts

1. How has menopause changed the way I see myself?
2. What practices help me feel grounded and whole in this new phase?
3. Where am I still holding onto shame or fear around aging?
4. How can I give myself more grace, not less, during this sacred shift?

Sacred Reflections: Your Notes

_____
_____
_____
_____
_____
_____
_____
_____
_____
_____
_____

The Sacred Journey

The Sacred Shift: Menopause with Grace

Chapter 6
Redefining Success: Retirement and Career Transitions

"If you want to make God laugh, tell Him your plans."
— Old Proverb

There's a certain rhythm to success we're taught to follow. Work hard. Climb steadily. Retire when the time feels "right." But life, in all its divine mystery, doesn't always honor our calendars.

Retirement—especially a second one—can feel like both a celebration and a reckoning. You look back at everything you've given, everything you've sacrificed, everything you've endured. You begin to ask: Was it worth it? Who am I now? What happens next?

I had my plans. I was going to retire on my own terms, in my own time. But the world shifted. The environment I had once served with pride began to change in ways that made staying feel like shrinking. And that's when I heard the whisper: It's time.

So I made the decision. Not just to retire—but to release.

And that's where this sacred chapter begins:
Not in the loss of a title, but in the rediscovery of truth.

When Success Starts to Feel Like a Straitjacket

There comes a moment in every accomplished woman's life when the accolades feel hollow and the calendar feels heavy. You look around and wonder how much of your worth was tied to your work. And how much of your identity was stitched into systems that no longer see you.

Retirement can stir unexpected grief. But it also offers space. Space to:

- Rethink your definition of purpose
- Reconnect with passions that were pushed aside
- Reimagine your life not by metrics, but by meaning

One chapter closing doesn't mean failure. It means freedom.

Self-Care in the Sacred Pivot

Sacred self-care during a career transition includes:

- Letting go of the need to explain your decision to everyone
- Allowing yourself to rest—truly rest—for the first time in decades
- Creating new routines that serve your spirit, not your schedule
- Holding space for grief, joy, and gratitude to co-exist
- Trusting that what feels like an ending is actually divine redirection

This wasn't just retirement. It was realignment. A release from what no longer fit, so I could rise into what God was calling me to next.

Scripture

"Commit your work to the Lord, and your plans will be established." — Proverbs 16:3

This verse reminds us that success isn't just about achievement—it's about alignment. When we offer our work, our seasons, and our surrender to God, He reshapes the plan for something far greater than we could imagine.

Thinking About Legacy

If the next generation of women watched how you left your job, what would they learn?
Would they see that leaving isn't failure—it's faith?
Would they learn that success is not about staying, but about knowing when to go?
Would they understand that transitions can be holy ground, not just hard roads?

Reflection Prompts

1. How has my definition of success evolved over the years?
2. What beliefs about work and worth do I need to release?
3. Where is God inviting me to rest, realign, or reinvent?
4. What do I want this next chapter to feel like—and how can I begin shaping it?

Sacred Reflections: Your Notes

_____
_____
_____
_____
_____
_____
_____
_____
_____
_____
_____
_____

The Sacred Journey

Redefining Success: Retirement and Career Transitions

Chapter 7
The Evolving Circle: When Friendships Fade

"Some people are in your life for a season, some for a reason, and some for a lifetime." — Unknown

There's a quiet kind of grief that comes with outgrowing a friendship. No funeral. No final conversation. Just a shift. A space. A silence that grows louder with time.

Friendships—especially those forged in your 20s, 30s, and 40s—feel like soul contracts. You imagine they'll last forever. You share secrets, raise children side by side, walk through marriages, divorces, illnesses. And then one day... something changes. A call doesn't come. A text goes unanswered. The connection, once easy and electric, becomes strained—or still.

And it hurts. Deeply.

I remember when my own friendships started shifting. At first, I thought I had done something wrong. I questioned whether I had been present enough, loving enough, available enough. I replayed conversations in my head, wondering if I missed a signal or failed a test I didn't know

I was taking. The grief was real. I felt the loss like a phantom limb.

Even though I understood the whole season, reason, lifetime thing, my heart still needed time to catch up with my head. And in that space, I realized this:

Friendship endings don't always come from betrayal. Sometimes, they come from becoming.

We grow. They grow. And not every version of us is meant to walk together forever. Some friendships are chapters, not the whole book—and that's okay.

Sometimes, letting go is a holy act. Not of abandonment— but of alignment.

And as I let go, I started to see who was still standing right beside me—some of them had been there all along.

Women who have walked and continue to walk beside me in sisterhood, legacy, and love, like Linda and Jolanda (who is with us in spirit), my beautiful best friends for ever and ever from junior high school; Regina, my sister-in-law and my nieces Nikita and Genesis; my cousin Jenny and my dear friend Siddy, who are both like big sisters to me; my dear friend and celebrity designer Lizz Russell; my mentors/friends KC McClain and Westanna Bobbitt, who is also my soror; my Sisters 4 Eva Jean, Elaine, Shiggy, Carmen, and Freddie; my loving Delta Sigma Theta Incorporated sorors Audra and Kimberly, and my beloved Line Sisters and Sands, 14 Grams of Gold Spring 1987, Inez, Stephanie, Ingrid, Cheryl, Ni aka Ivory, Faith, Terry Mamie, Margret, Priscilla, Kathleen, Karen, and Sharon,

Beta Eta Chapter, Alabama State University; and my daughter Rachel, whose fierce love and fresh wisdom often guide me more than she knows.

Special shout out to my brother Randall, who knows me in a way only someone who's grown up beside you can and always shows up for me with love and loyalty.

And of course, my mother, Betty Jo Lewis Walker Webb. Even in her dementia, she continues to be a source of encouragement joy, and sacred strength. She has always been my best friend—my heart's home.

And then, there were my furry girls—Rena and Mimi—both of whom have now crossed the Rainbow Bridge. Rena, my first little soul companion, was by my side from high school through early motherhood, a gentle, wise presence before I even had the words to describe what I needed. And Mimi? Mimi came at just the right time, when Rachel was seven, and she never left my side. Through divorce, single parenting, and the empty nest years, she reminded me what loyalty and unconditional love looked like. Their paws may have been small, but their impact was immense. And now, Raven—my brother's pup who visits regularly—brings her own little sparkle to my world, just when I need a laugh or a little light. Love doesn't always speak in words. Sometimes, it just curls up at your feet.

These are the people who really know me. Who see my heart. Who don't require explanations or performance. And for a while, I almost overlooked them while I was mourning what was lost.

But love doesn't always arrive in the way we expect. Sometimes, the most sacred friendships are the ones rooted in blood, in time, in history. And when we open our eyes to that kind of steady love—it changes everything.

Self-Care When Circles Shift

The evolution of friendships is part of our sacred becoming. But it's okay to admit: even when it's not personal, it feels personal.

Sacred self-care might include:

- Allowing yourself to grieve the loss of shared history
- Releasing the need to assign blame or find closure
- Journaling your gratitude for what that friendship once gave you
- Making space for new, aligned connections without forcing them
- Reminding yourself that your worth is not tied to someone else's availability

Scripture

"Two are better than one... If either of them falls down, one can help the other up." — Ecclesiastes 4:9-10

This verse reminds us that friendship is sacred, but it also changes shape. Some companions are with us for a lifetime. Others lift us just when we need it and then move on. Both are a blessing. Both are part of God's design.

Thinking About Legacy

If your daughter or granddaughter watched how you handled changing friendships, what would she learn?
Would she see that release can be done with grace?
Would she learn to honor both the bond and the boundary?
Would she feel permission to grieve, grow, and still open her heart again?

The Evolving Circle: When Friendships Fade

Reflection Prompts
1. What friendships have quietly faded, and what have I learned from them?
2. Where am I still holding on—and what might it look like to lovingly let go?
3. How do I want to be loved and supported in friendship moving forward?
4. Where am I being called to expand my circle—or tend to my solitude?

Sacred Reflections: Your Notes

_____

_____

_____

_____

_____

_____

_____

_____

_____

_____

_____

_____

The Sacred Journey

The Evolving Circle: When Friendships Fade

Chapter 8
Caregiving as a Sacred Calling

"To care for those who once cared for us is one of the highest honors." — Tia Walker

Caregiving changes everything. Your schedule. Your sleep. Your soul.

It is one of the most sacred, humbling, and exhausting roles a person can step into—and often, we do it without fanfare or recognition. Not because it's easy. But because love calls, and we answer.

For me, caregiving became a full chapter of my life—not a moment, but a rhythm. As my mother, began her journey with dementia, I found myself slowly becoming the keeper of memories, the advocate at appointments, the one who answers the same question with the same soft tone... again and again.

Some days, she knows exactly who I am. Other days, she drifts. But her spirit? Her spirit is still strong. She is still my mother. Still my best friend. Still one of the wisest women I know.

Caregiving revealed a love that stretches beyond convenience. It's a love that wakes up tired and keeps going. That cries in secret and smiles in service. That gives not because it has excess, but because it has purpose.

Caregiving Takes Many Forms

We often picture caregiving as a daughter tending to an aging mother. And while that's true for many, the picture is so much broader.

It's a husband caring for a wife whose body is changing from illness or age.
It's a son tending gently to his mother's needs, navigating pride and vulnerability.
It's a daughter caring for her father, shifting the dynamic of protection and provision.

Each scenario carries its own unique beauty and its own set of challenges—emotional, physical, relational. There are unspoken griefs in watching someone you love diminish. There is sacred tension in having to parent your parent, or nurse your partner, or sit with your own limitations as a child or spouse when you can't make them better.

And while we're caring, it's easy to forget this one, unshakable truth:
If we don't care for ourselves, we may not be here to finish the journey.

Caregiver burnout is real. Too many women collapse under the weight of invisible labor—but for Black women, that labor is often heavier, less acknowledged, and more expected. And yet we show up. We keep going. We sacrifice. But if we don't pause, nourish, rest, and release, we can end up burying ourselves before the ones we're trying to care for.

That's not selfishness. That's sacred awareness.

And When They Pass...

For those who have lost someone they were caring for, a different kind of grief emerges. It's not just the loss of a loved one. It's the loss of a role. A daily purpose. A relationship built around rhythms of need.

It can be disorienting.
You may feel relief—and then guilt.
You may feel sadness—and then emptiness.
You may not know who you are without the weight of care.

Let yourself feel it. Mourn the person and the pattern. Because caregiving isn't something you just turn off. It becomes part of who you are.

And yet, even after loss, the love you gave doesn't disappear. It becomes legacy. It becomes memory. It becomes the way you show up for yourself moving forward.

Sacred Self-Care in the Caregiver's Role

Self-care during caregiving isn't luxury—it's lifeline.

Sacred self-care means:

- Releasing guilt when you need rest
- Accepting help without apology

- Speaking up when you feel invisible or overwhelmed
- Creating small rituals just for you—even if they're brief
- Recognizing that fatigue, frustration, and grief are all valid
- Trusting that you are doing enough, even when it doesn't feel like it

You are allowed to need care, too. Even while giving it.

Scripture

"Even to your old age and gray hairs I am he, I am he who will sustain you." — Isaiah 46:4

This verse reminds us that God is not only walking with the one we're caring for—He is walking with us, too. He sees the labor. He knows the load. And He sustains us through it all.

Thinking About Legacy

If your children or grandchildren watched how you showed up as a caregiver, what would they learn?
Would they see that care is holy, not thankless?
Would they witness that boundaries and love can co-exist?
Would they feel empowered to ask for help—and offer it—without shame?

The Sacred Journey

Reflection Prompts

1. What version of myself has emerged through caregiving?
2. Where do I need support, and how can I open myself to receive it?
3. What grief am I holding that I haven't yet acknowledged?
4. How can I honor the one I care for and honor myself?

A Gentle Invitation

If this chapter speaks to your current season, I invite you to go deeper with my published caregiver's journal—a sacred space filled with affirmations, reflection prompts, and encouragement for women who are carrying so much with grace. Because your heart deserves tending, too.

Sacred Reflections: Your Notes

_____

_____

_____

_____

_____

_____

Caregiving as a Sacred Calling

The Sacred Journey

PART II

SACRED WHOLENESS: RETURNING TO YOURSELF

Chapter 9
Vitality Reimagined

*"I do not wish to shrink myself for the comfort of others.
I want to expand—body, soul, and presence."*
— Unknown

At this stage in life, vitality becomes less about appearance and more about alignment.

It's not about fitting into the jeans from ten years ago—it's about fitting into a life that feels good from the inside out. For women over 50, vitality isn't defined by weight loss goals or restrictive routines. It's defined by joy, movement, softness, strength, and peace in our own skin.

We've spent too many years measuring our worth by the number on a scale, the firmness of a waistline, or the ability to "bounce back." But real vitality? It's in the bounce forward.

My Own Reimagining

I used to believe that vitality meant energy, performance, productivity. That I had to do more, be more, push harder. But now, I understand it differently.

Vitality, for me, is in the slowness. The intentionality. The stretch of a morning walk. The breath I take before I respond. The softness I allow without apology. I'm still working on my health goals, still learning how to move in ways that honor my body—but I no longer chase wellness like a punishment.

I invite it in as a prayer.

Because feeling good in your body is not a vanity project—it's a victory.

Reclaiming Wholeness

Vitality is not a number—it's a feeling. A flow. A rhythm of life that comes from within.

And let me be real—this journey hasn't been linear. I remember crying in the doctor's office the day I was told I had high blood pressure. I thought I was doing everything right. Then the next visit, my numbers were great… but my cholesterol was up. It felt like I couldn't win.

And don't even get me started on the knees. There's a phenomenon no one warns you about—how your joints start speaking to you every time you climb the stairs. Or how a full night's sleep turns into a series of bathroom breaks. Or how your eyelashes, eyebrows, and hair start thinning at the edges, almost like they're slowly tiptoeing away.

And then, of course, the little roll right under your arm that didn't used to be there. The gentle back fat that shows up like an uninvited guest in fitted dresses. These are the realities of a body that's shifting, aging, becoming.

But they're also signs that we are alive—and still evolving.

Vitality doesn't mean nothing changes. It means we listen to the changes and love ourselves through them. It means laughing at what surprises us, blessing what aches, and still claiming joy in movement, softness in strength, and reverence in rest.

Sacred self-care for vitality might include:

- Releasing toxic beliefs about weight and aging
- Moving your body in joyful, unforced ways
- Drinking water like it's holy (because it is)
- Reclaiming rest as part of your health plan
- Choosing foods that nourish rather than restrict
- Laughing, dancing, stretching, and breathing deeply
- Listening to your body like you would listen to a friend

You are not too old. You are right on time. And every step you take toward wholeness—whether physical, emotional, or spiritual—is sacred.

Scripture

> *"Do you not know that your bodies are temples of the Holy Spirit... You are not your own; you were bought at a price. Therefore, honor God with your bodies."*
> — 1 Corinthians 6:19-20

This verse reminds us that caring for our bodies is not vanity—it's worship. We move, nourish, and rest not to shrink ourselves, but to steward the vessel we've been entrusted with.

Thinking About Legacy

If your daughter or granddaughter watched how you treated your body, what would she learn?
Would she see joy or judgment?
Would she learn that self-care is sacred?
Would she grow up understanding that beauty has no age—and vitality is a birthright?

Reflection Prompts

1. What does vitality look and feel like for me right now?
2. What beliefs about health or beauty do I need to release?
3. How can I move my body in ways that bring joy, not punishment?
4. Where am I still shrinking—and where am I ready to expand?

Sacred Reflections: Your Notes

_____

_____

_____

_____

_____

The Sacred Journey

Vitality Reimagined

Chapter 10
Emotional Resilience

"I am not what happened to me. I am what I choose to become." — Carl Jung

Some storms come with warnings. Others show up unannounced and rearrange your entire life.

Divorce. Betrayal. Disappointment. Workplace politics. Loneliness. The heartbreak of watching people you trusted fall short—or walk away.

Emotional resilience doesn't mean you didn't break. It means you learned how to breathe through the breaking and rise anyway.

When I Chose to Stand Back Up

I've had to be resilient more times than I can count.

When my marriage ended, I didn't just grieve the relationship—I grieved the dream. The identity. The story I thought I was still writing. And just when I thought I had found steady ground, another storm came: betrayal at work.

The kind that makes you question not just your job, but your worth. When you've shown up, poured in, been the example—and you're still dismissed, silenced, or used as a scapegoat.

I cried. I questioned everything. And still, I rose.

Not because I wanted to be strong—but because I had to be. And that's when I began to understand resilience is not about armor. It's about alignment.

The Superwoman Curse

So many women are praised for their strength. But that strength has a shadow. For Black women, that shadow has long been misinterpreted as independence without need, or resilience without rest.

We're taught to wear the cape, hold the line, dry our own tears, and never let anyone see us crumble.

But here's the truth: the Superwoman role is a survival tool. Not a soul strategy.

It helps us function. It gets us through. But it also exhausts us, isolates us, and sometimes, slowly erases the parts of us that long for softness, rest, and truth.

You are not weak because you're tired. You are not dramatic because you need a break. And you are not angry just because you raise your voice or show emotion.

Grief Doesn't Always Look Like Tears

One of the cruelest misunderstandings placed on Black women is the assumption that our pain is anger. That our expressions of hurt, disappointment, or fear are threatening or overreactions.

But sometimes, we're grieving. Sometimes, we're scared. Sometimes, we're ashamed. And often, we're just tired.

Emotional resilience means naming your feelings. It means not having to mask your sorrow as silence. It means creating room for your full humanity.

It's the strength to:

- Go to therapy
- End toxic relationships
- Say "no more" and mean it
- Rest without guilt
- Weep when needed—and laugh just as freely
- Let go of roles that were never meant to define you

Scripture

> *"We are hard pressed on every side, but not crushed; perplexed, but not in despair... struck down, but not destroyed."* — 2 Corinthians 4:8-9

This verse is a mirror to the lived experience of so many strong women. We are allowed to be pressed. To be perplexed. To even feel knocked down. But by the grace of God, we are not destroyed.

Thinking About Legacy

If the next generation of women watched how you navigated emotional pain, what would they learn?
Would they see that vulnerability is not weakness?
Would they learn that strength includes softness?
Would they witness a woman who honored her heart—not just her responsibilities?

Reflection Prompts

1. What storms have I survived that I haven't fully acknowledged?
2. Where have I been praised for being strong—but needed someone to check on my heart?
3. What emotions have I been masking as "fine"?
4. How can I allow myself to soften without shame?

Sacred Reflections: Your Notes

The Sacred Journey

Emotional Resilience

Chapter 11
Sacred Alignment

"Almost everything will work again if you unplug it for a few minutes... including you." — Anne Lamott

Have you ever arrived home and realized you couldn't remember the drive?

You made every turn. Obeyed every light. Pulled into your driveway. But the details? The presence? Gone. Your body was there—but your mind was somewhere else entirely.

That's what living on autopilot can feel like.

So many of us move through life like that—checking boxes, keeping appointments, doing what we "should." But alignment? Alignment asks a different question:

Does this still serve me? Does this still reflect who I am becoming?

From Spending Time to Investing Time

For years, I spent my time.
On obligations. On shoulds. On autopilot.

But then I learned to invest my time.
In people who fed my spirit.
In work that aligned with my calling.
In moments that brought me peace.

There is a sacred difference between spending time and investing it. One drains. The other plants seeds. Alignment means being intentional with your time—not just busy. Present—not just productive.

The Day I Began to Notice

When I was going through my divorce, I started walking outside. At first, it was just about movement—trying to clear my head. But something shifted.

I started to notice.

The way the light hit a certain patch of grass. The rhythm of the trees swaying. The sound of a bird that seemed to call only when I passed. It was as if nature was calling out to me—asking me to be still, to be present, to see again.

It reminded me of that powerful line from *The Color Purple:*

> "I think it pisses God off when you walk by the color purple in a field and don't notice it."

That was me. I had walked past the beauty of my own life for too long. Alignment began when I noticed again. When I realized that everything around me was trying to bring me back to myself—and back to God.

Self-Care for Sacred Alignment

Alignment isn't about perfection. It's about presence. About honoring the pace, the peace, and the pull of your purpose.

Sacred self-care might include:

- Unplugging from technology for an hour a day to reconnect with your spirit
- Journaling each morning with the question: "What does alignment look like for me today?"
- Taking nature walks without a destination—just to listen
- Reassessing commitments: Do they reflect who I am now?
- Lighting a candle and praying before major decisions
- Scheduling margin—not just meetings—on your calendar

Scripture

"In all your ways acknowledge Him, and He will direct your path." — Proverbs 3:6

This verse reminds us that alignment is not just about clarity—it's about surrender. When we move through life acknowledging God at every step, He doesn't just bless the journey—He becomes the compass.

Thinking About Legacy

If someone watched how you structured your day, what would they learn?
Would they see a woman who knows how to pause?
Would they witness a life rooted in purpose, not performance?

Would they feel inspired to slow down, align, and listen for the voice of God?

Reflection Prompts
1. Where in my life am I operating on autopilot?
2. What does it look like to invest my time instead of just spending it?
3. What does my body, spirit, and schedule reveal about my current alignment?
4. What helps me return to presence—and how can I create more of it?

Sacred Reflections: Your Notes

_____

_____

_____

_____

_____

_____

_____

_____

_____

The Sacred Journey

Sacred Alignment

Chapter 12
Rediscovering You

"And the day came when the risk to remain tight in a bud was more painful than the risk it took to blossom."
— Anaïs Nin

Let's make something plain.

If Sacred Alignment is about how you move through the world—with intention, presence, and divine direction—then Rediscovering You is about who you are when the world goes quiet. When the roles fall away. When you finally have time to ask, What do I want? Who am I becoming now?

This chapter is not about reinvention—it's about reintroduction.

You've spent years showing up for everyone else. Now it's time to come home to you.

This is the Chapter I've Been Waiting For

As I step into my second retirement, this is the part of the journey I'm most looking forward to.

Not just resting—but rediscovering.
Not just releasing—but remembering.
Not just starting over—but starting deeper.

There are pieces of me I never had time to fully explore. Passions I've silenced. Dreams I've set aside for practicality. Softness I've hidden to survive.

But now? Now I get to look for myself again.
In the quiet.
In the joy.
In the everyday.

The Woman Beneath the Roles

For so long, I was daughter.
Wife.
Mother.
Air Force Officer.
Leader.
Caregiver.
Coach.

But who am I when no one is watching? Who is the woman beneath the titles?

Rediscovery is not about answers. It's about curiosity. It's a sacred invitation to explore the things that light you up now—not who you were in your 30s, not who people expect you to be.

Who are you, really? What do you enjoy when no one needs anything from you?

Self-Care for Rediscovery

Rediscovery takes time—but it also takes trust. You won't find all the answers in a week. But you will begin to hear your own voice again.

Sacred self-care might include:

- Creating a "joy list" of things that make you feel alive
- Taking yourself on artist or soul dates—solo time to explore what lights you up
- Revisiting childhood passions and noticing what still calls to you
- Decluttering not just your home, but your calendar—making space for exploration
- Journaling the question: Who am I now? every week for a month
- Trying one new thing a month—just for the sake of play

You don't have to start over to discover something new. You just have to show up for yourself—on purpose.

And let this be your reminder:
It is not too late.
Not to grow.
Not to dream.
Not to love yourself in a new way.
You are not behind—you are right on time.
And everything you need to become who you were always meant to be is already within you.

Scripture

"Behold, I am doing a new thing! Now it springs up; do you not perceive it?" — Isaiah 43:19

This verse reminds us that God doesn't stop creating. And that includes you. You are not done becoming. There is still newness, softness, joy, and divine beauty waiting to emerge.

Thinking About Legacy

If your daughter or granddaughter watched you rediscover yourself, what would she learn?
Would she see that life doesn't end at 50—it expands?
Would she learn that it's never too late to begin again?
Would she witness a woman willing to meet herself in every season?

Reflection Prompts

1. What parts of myself have I forgotten—or ignored?
2. What brings me joy now that I never made room for before?
3. Who am I becoming now that I have space to ask?
4. What do I want to try, explore, or express—just for me?

Sacred Reflections: Your Notes

The Sacred Journey

Chapter 13
Love at Every Stage

"Age does not protect you from love. But love, to some extent, protects you from age." — Anaïs Nin

Love changes—but it never loses its sacredness.

In our 20s, love may have looked like butterflies and potential.
In our 30s, it may have looked like building a life.
In our 40s, it may have been tested—through stress, loss, betrayal, or silence.
And now? In our 50s, 60s, and beyond—love begins to look like truth.

Love becomes less about the fairytale and more about freedom.
Less about chemistry and more about connection.
Less about what we can prove and more about what we can feel without fear.

Love That Evolves With You

As you grow, love must grow, too. Not everyone who loved you at one stage can meet you in the next. And not every version of love you accepted before will serve the woman you are now.

But don't let that scare you. Let it liberate you.

Because love at this stage is no longer about filling voids—it's about reflecting wholeness. It's less about being chosen, and more about choosing yourself first—and welcoming someone who celebrates that.

Different Forms, Sacred Ground

Love isn't just romantic.

It's in the sister-friend who checks on you without you asking.
In the dog who curls up at your feet like home.
In the late-night laughter with your grown daughter.
In the prayer whispered over someone you'll never meet.

Love is layered. It's lived. And it's always sacred.

Self-Care for Love at Every Stage

Whether you are single, partnered, divorced, widowed, or open to love again, you can care for your heart with sacred intention.

Self-care might include:

- Writing a love letter to yourself for the woman you are becoming
- Revisiting your love values: What do I want now? What do I need to feel safe?
- Creating rituals for self-nurturing: long baths, good books, slow mornings
- Surrounding yourself with people who pour into you, not drain you

- Taking yourself on solo dates to remember your own beauty and company
- Choosing softness without apology—especially when the world tells you to harden

Scripture

"Above all, clothe yourselves with love, which binds everything together in perfect harmony."
— Colossians 3:14

Love is the sacred thread that ties it all together. It holds space for grace, growth, and gentle becoming. And at every age, in every form, love is still yours to give and receive.

Thinking About Legacy

If your daughter or granddaughter watched how you loved—yourself and others—what would she learn?
Would she see that love is not about desperation, but discernment?
Would she learn that love doesn't end—it evolves?
Would she witness a woman who loved from overflow, not emptiness?

Reflection Prompts
1. What have I learned about love through the different stages of my life?
2. Where do I still need healing in how I love or allow myself to be loved?
3. How can I show myself love in tangible, sacred ways this season?
4. What kind of love do I want to attract, welcome, or nurture moving forward?

Sacred Reflections: Your Notes

The Sacred Journey

Love at Every Stage

PART III

SACRED LEGACY: LIVING AND LEAVING A LIFE THAT TEACHES

Chapter 14
Life in Harmony

"Happiness is when what you think, what you say, and what you do are in harmony." — Mahatma Gandhi

Let's begin with a truth:

Harmony is not balance.
Balance is about equal parts. Harmony is about peaceful coexistence. It's the art of letting things take their rightful place—without forcing them to be equal or perfect.

At this stage of life, harmony matters more than hustle.
It's not about doing everything.
It's about holding everything with grace.
It's about flowing between roles, emotions, seasons, and callings—without losing yourself in the noise.

Living Harmony, Not Just Talking About It

This chapter isn't about organizing your calendar—it's about honoring your capacity.

Harmony might mean:

- Saying no without guilt
- Letting some things remain undone
- Asking for help
- Blocking time for joy—not just productivity
- Trusting that God fills the gaps we can't

Harmony is holy. It's the place where your soul, your body, your emotions, and your calling begin to hum in quiet agreement.

How It's Different from Sacred Alignment

While Sacred Alignment is about being present and intentional in the moment—how you walk through life with God and discernment—Life in Harmony is about the ongoing rhythm of your full life. It's the symphony of your past, your healing, your relationships, your future. It's about how you live with all of it—without needing every part to be perfectly resolved.

Harmony is the soft yes. The holy pause. The understanding that you are a whole woman, not a compartment.

Harmony in Real Life

Harmony might look like:

- Listening to your body and canceling plans
- Keeping a quiet Sabbath once a month
- Embracing your ambition and your need for rest
- Laughing while grieving
- Holding gratitude and longing at the same time
- Loving someone while letting them go

Harmony doesn't mean everything is easy. It means everything is yours to hold with grace.

Self-Care for Life in Harmony

Sacred self-care might include:

- Creating morning or evening rituals that nourish your spirit
- Having a "sacred pause" practice before making new commitments
- Using music, aromatherapy, or prayer to center your energy each day
- Making space for solitude and stillness—even for just ten minutes
- Scheduling joy the way you schedule meetings

Scripture

> *"Let the peace of Christ rule in your hearts... and be thankful."* — Colossians 3:15

This verse reminds us that peace is not just a feeling—it's a ruler. When peace is in charge, harmony can flourish. And when gratitude is present, we see our lives more clearly.

Thinking About Legacy

If your daughter, granddaughter, or mentee watched how you moved through your days, what would she learn?
Would she learn to pause without apology?
Would she see a woman whose life is full—but not frantic?
Would she witness that harmony is a sacred rhythm—not a fragile balancing act?

Reflection Prompts

1. What areas of my life feel in harmony right now—and which feel dissonant?
2. How can I begin to embrace rhythm over perfection?
3. What does it look like to hold all parts of my story with grace?
4. Where do I need to invite more stillness, softness, or space?

Sacred Reflections: Your Notes

_____
_____
_____
_____
_____
_____
_____
_____
_____
_____
_____

The Sacred Journey

Life in Harmony

Chapter 15
Living Sacredly Through Life's Seasons

"To everything there is a season, and a time for every purpose under heaven." — Ecclesiastes 3:1

There is a rhythm to life that doesn't always ask for permission.
It shifts. It surprises. It calls us forward—or slows us down—without waiting for us to feel ready.

And yet, there is something holy about surrendering to the season we're in.

When you live sacredly, you stop fighting the changes and start listening to them.

Sacred Living Isn't Seasonal—But It Honors the Seasons

Some seasons are for blooming.
Some are for pruning.
Some are for resting.
And some are for replanting the seeds you forgot you carried.

Living sacredly means:

- Embracing the wisdom of your now
- Releasing the pressure to be who you were ten years ago
- Welcoming the quiet as much as the calling
- Seeing God not just in your progress, but in your pauses

This is Not the End. It's the Evolution.

You are still growing—even if the growth looks quieter now.
You are still learning—even if your classroom is life itself.
And you are still sacred—even when the mirror shows gray where there once was color, softness where there once was urgency.

Living sacredly is the legacy. It's what we pass down to daughters, granddaughters, and sisters, nieces and friends. Not a perfect life. Not an easy one. But one that honors the sacred at every stage.

Self-Care for Living Through the Seasons

Sacred self-care for this final rhythm might include:

- Creating an annual reflection ritual around your birthday or a milestone
- Letting yourself grieve aging while still celebrating it
- Wearing clothes that feel like softness and power at the same time

- Making peace with what no longer fits—and blessing what does
- Asking yourself gently: What is this season teaching me?

Scripture

"The righteous will flourish like a palm tree... they will still bear fruit in old age, they will stay fresh and green."
— Psalm 92:12, 14

This verse reminds us that sacred living doesn't expire. You are still fruitful. Still relevant. Still radiant in God's eyes. You are not done—and neither is He.

Thinking About Legacy

If your life was the model someone else used for growing older, what would they learn?
Would they learn to resist change—or to lean into it?
Would they see aging as a loss—or as a sacred unveiling?
Would they feel permission to slow down, let go, and live fully in the season they're in?

Reflection Prompts

1. What season of life am I in—and what is it teaching me?
2. What do I need to release in order to live more freely and sacredly now?
3. What rituals or rhythms help me stay anchored through change?
4. How do I want to be remembered—not just for what I did, but for how I lived?

Sacred Reflections: Your Notes

The Sacred Journey

Living Sacredly Through Life's Seasons

Closing Reflections
You Are the Sacred Journey

If you've made it to this point in the book, I want you to know this:

You didn't just read a book.

You walked a path.

You made room for truth.

You softened into grace.

You remembered what the world tried to make you forget—

that you are the sacred journey.

This book was never about fixing you.

It was about finding you.

Honoring you.

And reminding you that even in the shifting seasons, the shedding, the silence—

you are still whole.

You are still wise.

You are still worthy.

You are not too late.
You are not too much.
You are exactly who you were created to be—becoming more of her with every breath.

Final Prayer

God, thank You for the woman reading these words.
For her courage, her questions, her quiet strength.
Thank You for the seasons that tried to break her—and instead built her.
Thank You for the softness she is reclaiming.
For the boundaries she is learning to hold.
For the joy she is no longer apologizing for.
For the faith that's deeper than before.
Bless her as she continues this sacred journey—not just as a reader, but as a living, breathing testimony of grace.
May she walk forward with light in her eyes, peace in her heart, and purpose in her steps.
Amen.

Final Affirmation

I am the journey and the destination.

I walk with wisdom, with wonder, and with a heart wide open.

I do not need to be perfect to be powerful.

I honor my pace.

I trust my process.

And I show up for my sacred self—again and again.

Book Club Questions

1. Which chapter spoke to you the most—and why?
   Was it tied to a season you're currently navigating or one with which you've finally made peace?

2. How has your definition of self-care changed after reading this book?
   What does sacred self-care look like for you now?

3. What parts of yourself have you reclaimed, softened, or redefined during this journey?
   Were there any surprises?

4. In what ways has your faith helped you navigate life's transitions?
   Are there any scriptures or prayers you return to in uncertain times?

5. What does emotional resilience mean to you at this stage of life?
   Where do you still feel pressure to be the "strong one"?

6. Which chapter challenged you the most?
   Did anything make you pause, reflect, or feel uncomfortable in a productive way?

Book Club Questions

7. What boundaries are you learning to set—or protect?
   How does honoring your boundaries shift the way you love yourself and others?

8. What does love look like to you now compared to ten or twenty years ago?
   How are you opening yourself to love at this stage of life?

9. What legacy do you want to leave for the women who come after you?
   What wisdom are you ready to pass on?

10. What is your next sacred step?
    After reading this book, what are you being called to do, release, embrace, or become?

11. How do we hold space for one another with compassion especially when we're all navigating our own transitions?
    What does true emotional presence look and feel like in a world where overwhelm is common?

The Sacred Self-Care Toolkit

"Don't be afraid. Be focused. Be determined. Be hopeful. Be empowered." — Michelle Obama

This is not just a toolkit—it's a permission slip.

To rest. To rise. To reflect. To rediscover joy.

Each practice below is an offering—gentle, soulful, and sacred.

Choose what speaks to you in the moment. Leave what doesn't. Return as needed.

When You Need Stillness

- Sit in silence for 5–10 minutes, hands over your heart, whispering, "I am safe. I am here."
- Light a candle and play soft instrumental music while doing nothing else.
- Take a slow walk without headphones—let nature speak.

- Create a "Sacred Pause" corner in your home with a journal, blanket, and tea.
- Internally recite a breath prayer. Inhale: "I receive peace." Exhale: "I release worry."

When You Feel Overwhelmed

- Do a "brain release" journal dump—write without editing for 10 minutes.
- Touch something real: water, your favorite lotion, the earth.
- Create a "Do Less" list—3 things you're letting go of today.
- Play a 3-song dance break playlist (just for you).
- Say no. Full sentence. No explanation.

When You're Grieving or Releasing

- Write a letter to what you've lost—and burn it (safely) or bury it.
- Create a small altar with a photo, candle, or object of meaning.
- Let tears fall while holding your own hand.
- Listen to a song that mirrors your emotion and sing it out loud.

- Speak this aloud: "I am allowed to grieve. I am allowed to heal. I am still whole."

When You're Reclaiming Joy

- Plan a joy date just for yourself: bookstore, café, park, art exhibit.
- Keep a "delight list"—write one thing daily that made you smile.
- Revisit a childhood hobby (coloring, puzzles, dancing in socks).
- Buy yourself flowers—for no reason at all.
- Speak blessings over your reflection: "You are beautiful. You are beloved. You are becoming."

When You're Preparing to Shift or Grow

- Ask yourself: What am I being called to release? What am I being called to rise into?
- Create a playlist for your next chapter—songs that feel like freedom.
- Write a "Letter to My Future Self" and date it for 6 months from now.
- Do a sacred decluttering of one drawer, shelf, or inbox.
- Pray over your calendar: "God, guide my yes, protect my no."

To Hold Space for Others[1]

- Lead with curiosity not assumptions. Ask how they would like to be supported.
- Resist the urge to compare. Pain is not competitive.
- Practice reflective listening. Sometimes, the gift is simply being heard.
- Honor timing. Just because someone shares doesn't mean they want immediate feedback or advice.
- Tend to your own overwhelm. You can't offer what you don't have. Self-regulation is part of sacred community care.

---

[1] Holding space is the art of being present with someone without judgment, rescue, or agenda. It's listening with the heart, witnessing with humility, and offering love without needing to fix.

Six Core Types of Self-Care

1. Physical Self-Care

   Nourishing your body with movement, rest, hydration, and mindful attention.

2. Emotional Self-Care

   Honoring your feelings, processing emotions, and creating space for healing.

3. Mental Self-Care

   Stimulating your mind with reflection, learning, and mental clarity.

4. Spiritual Self-Care

   Connecting with God through prayer, devotion, stillness, and spiritual practices.

5. Social/Relational Self-Care

   Nurturing life-giving relationships and establishing healthy boundaries.

6. Financial/Practical Self-Care

   Managing resources, planning wisely, and creating systems that support peace.

If you enjoyed *The Sacred Journey,* please tell a friend and leave a brief review at Amazon.

Thanks so much for your engagement and support.

Jolisa

About the Author

Jolisa Webb Dudley is a retired military officer, senior federal leader, certified personal growth and divorce coach, and the founder of Beauty in the Midst LLC. With a heart for women navigating transitions in midlife, she blends faith, wisdom, and lived experience into every offering. Her writing speaks to women who are ready to reclaim their voice, rewrite their narrative, and rise into their next chapter with clarity and grace.

She is the author of *Caregiver's Reflection Journal: A Sanctuary for Your Journey of Compassion, Resilience, and Self-Care*, available on Amazon—a heartfelt guide honoring the emotional, spiritual, and practical aspects of caregiving.

Jolisa is the proud mother of one daughter, a devoted caregiver, and a joyful witness to the healing power of sacred self-care.

www.ingramcontent.com/pod-product-compliance
Lightning Source LLC
Chambersburg PA
CBHW030222170426
43194CB00007BA/826